W

Lessons of the *Solas*

D. Marion Clark

What Matters © 2012 by D. Marion Clark

Unless otherwise indicated, Scripture quotations are from ESV Bible ® (The Holy Bible, English Standard Version ®). Copyright © 2001 by Crossway Bibles, a publishing ministry of Good News Publishers. Used by permission. All rights reserved.

ISBN-13: 978-1539680345
ISBN-10: 1539680347

Printed in the United States of America

In memory of two mentors of my faith: Richard Scheer and James Montgomery Boice

Table of Contents

Introduction
I Get It!

The work did not seem difficult. I merely had to dig a few more inches in the foundation ditch that a back-hoe had already dug three feet deep. The ditch was about sixty feet long, but how long could it take to shovel out inches of dirt? Longer and more difficult than I thought! The dirt turned out to be clay; my flat shovel could barely get a chip. I had to first use a pickaxe to break up the clay, then scoop it out with the shovel. This was going to take *forever!* Little by little I chipped at the clay and scooped. After a while I looked up and moaned over the distance I still had to go. Indeed, it appeared I had made little progress. But then I glanced behind me. Why, I had actually moved forward – farther than I had expected. I realized that if I kept to the task without worrying about how far I had to go, I would reach the goal.

This was one time when looking behind moved me forward to what was ahead.

This series of messages is my way of looking back. They are the significant lessons I have learned during my own spiritual pilgrimage concerning what matters. All but one came to me in "I get it!" moments that immediately changed my thinking, while the last one regarding grace was no less profound in shaping my spiritual growth and my ministry. Oddly enough, thinking through these messages led to an "I get it" moment. It dawned on me that my lessons reflected the ancient truths recovered by the Reformation known as the five *solas*. Here they are in my revised order:

Solus Christus (Christ Alone) – By the work of Christ alone we are saved. God has provided no other means for becoming reconciled with him other than through his Son.

Sola Fide (Faith Alone) – We do not "do our part" through good works to add on to the part Christ has done for salvation, nor do we earn God's favor by good works. We are justified by faith and live by faith alone.

Sola Scriptura (Scripture Alone) – Scripture alone is God's revelation. We are to trust it to teach us about God and what he wants of us. It alone is to be the measure for testing all other teachings and beliefs.

Soli Deo Gloria (For God's Glory Alone) – We and all creation exist for the purpose of glorifying God, who is working all things out for his glory.

Soli Gratia (Grace Alone) – Whatever faith we may exercise and good we may do is by the grace of God, who loves us not because of what we have done, but out of his own free will.

The ancient Preacher of Ecclesiastes stated in his day that "there is nothing new under the sun" (Eccles. 1:9). So I have learned, yet again, that my truth discoveries are nothing more than recovering for myself what our fathers and mothers of the faith discovered for themselves in each generation. Perhaps this was C. S. Lewis' reason for titling his allegorical conversion story *The Pilgrim's Regress*. Real progress is made by discovering truth that is not so much hidden as it is ignored. In my series of talks on *Speaking the Truth in Love*, I noted that I had no profound wisdom to pass on, simply the commonsense wisdom of the kitchen table; so I present nothing new in these

3

messages. They are merely an accounting of how I learned the age-old truths of the Gospel as expressed in the tenets of the Reformation.

Years ago I had such a re-finding experience with what is known as the means of grace. I was restless in my early years in the ministry, feeling that I was missing something experientially. I did not *feel* the power of God as I thought I should. What was I doing wrong? I looked at my Charismatic brethren who seemed to experience God every time they prayed and worshiped. Perhaps I needed to get baptized by the Holy Spirit like them. So I tried it. I did get more feeling, but I never spoke in tongues, and I could not get the "God told me" revelations that everyone else seemed to have on a regular basis. What was I lacking?

It was not until I began serving as an Associate Minister at Tenth Presbyterian Church under James Boice that the "I get it" understanding came. I was assigned the pastoral prayer for the morning services. I did not think too much about this. I did enjoy giving that prayer, and even now I find it to be my most fruitful prayer time. I think it has to do with praying audibly which helps me concentrate. Letting the psalm, which we read responsively earlier in the service, set the tone and content also made it particularly meaningful to me. Soon into those prayers I began to receive thanks from worshippers telling me how they were impacted by them. I was surprised to find that such ordinary means of praying could touch others deeply.

My next step of awakening came one day as I was studying scripture in preparation for a sermon. The thought occurred to me: When is it that I really do get excited about God? It is when I am grasping truth from his Word. I love to discover the treasure of a scripture text and to share that discovery. What I had wanted from personal revelation, God was giving me through his written Word.

The final step came when I was privileged to lead a weekly Communion service. There I saw the effect of this sacramental sign and seal on both the worshippers and me as it fed our faith and strengthened us spiritually. Week after week of preaching the Gospel, praying in response to the Gospel, and then communicating the sign of the

Gospel gave us comfort and inspired us to serve God with thankfulness and joy. The power of these "ordinary" activities was brought home to me one Sunday when I was asked to help a small church nearby with a baptism. I preached and conducted the Tenth Communion service, then traveled a few blocks for the other service. In one morning, I had led the congregation in prayer, preached, and administered the Lord's Supper and baptism. In each activity the Gospel was expressed, and my joy grew each time. In short, I learned the power of the ordinary means – Word, prayer, sacraments – by which our Lord ministers his grace to us. I had come home to the place where generations of Christians had been enjoying their God.

Such is my prayer for you – that you will delight in God as you read of these wanderings into the old fields of the *solas*. Greater saints than I have plowed these fields and produced rich insight, and so I hope my discoveries of "what matters" will whet your appetite to explore these truths more deeply.

Chapter 1
What Matters is Knowing Christ

I liked their music. I was seventeen. They were the first Christian band I had ever heard – a group of college and high school students singing the new folk-pop Christian music, including songs from the new musical *Godspell*. But there was something more. They spoke about knowing Jesus. There was something different about them.

I grew up in the Bible Belt where, at that time, everyone belonged to a church and professed to be a Christian. We all knew our Bible stories and, of course, the story about Jesus dying on the cross for us. And we all believed. I did not know anyone growing up who would have said he did not believe in God or, except for the small Jewish population in our town, that Jesus was God's Son. Even the "bad" kids would not have argued that Christianity was a lie. On the other hand, I did not know anyone my age for whom Christianity had special meaning. We went to church, but it had little impact on our daily lives. My friends and I were basically "good" kids who fit into the Christian church system.

The One Way young people were different though. They spoke and sang about Jesus as though they really did love him, as though he had made a difference in their lives. It struck me that it was possible not merely to believe a system but to know a Person. It was possible to know Jesus, not as a mere religious figure who did something for me, but who could be in me and with me.

"Prepare ye the way of the Lord," was the *Godspell* song playing in my mind later that evening as I walked home and came to the dreaded park that stood in the way. I could walk around the small enclosure as I normally did at night. Even into high school, walking in the dark alone unnerved me, particularly when walking by bushes or trees where anyone or anything could be hiding! But, I reasoned, if Jesus is with me (as I believed he was), I could walk through that park without fear. And so I went forward with "Prepare ye" in my mind. Halfway through I knew I would make it and cheerfully touched the dreaded trees. I actually made a point of brushing all the bushes on the way home! This is real. This idea of having a true relationship with Christ is real!

This testimony of believing on Jesus Christ is by no means a startling testimony. Nevertheless, it was my baptism into what the true Christian believer understands; whatever his experience may be – what matters is knowing Jesus. Or more to the point – what matters *is* Jesus.

My pilgrimage in my relationship with Jesus continued. Love for Christ was brought further home to me the following summer at Explo' 72. There I met thousands of Christians who expressed love and devotion to Jesus. In college I grew in understanding Jesus as more than a super friend who saved me. In a religion class, I read excerpts from Dietrich Bonhoeffer, who made the point that Jesus is not a bandage we use merely to help us out when we feel we need him. The InterVarsity books, retreats, and especially the InterVarsity leader Rich Scheer instilled in me a higher view of Christ as one to be worshipped as Lord, as well as loved as Savior.

It is this knowledge of who Jesus is and what he has done that binds us Christians together. I have heard dozens upon dozens of testimonies of persons from all walks of life – the Bible Belt Southerner like me, the Philadelphia street fighter, the Thai soldier, the Chinese scholar, the Turkish minister, the Jewish advertiser, the jungle tribesman. Our one common element is knowing and loving Jesus Christ.

I speak of my "I get it" moments of my spiritual pilgrimage. But the journey did not begin until that period in 1972 when through the three events – an April Billy Graham Crusade, the One Way concert, and Explo' 72 – that my first "I get it" insight came. What matters is Jesus and the work he did on the cross to redeem me from my sins. It was Jesus I prayed to receive at the crusade, Jesus whom Fred, Trish, Mark and the others in the band spoke passionately about. It was Jesus whose name was spoken of and praised throughout the Explo '72 youth conference. I was sitting in the Cotton Bowl stadium when I first heard the Scripture read which spoke to my own heart. Here it is in *The Living Bible* paraphrase used at that time:

> I don't understand myself at all, for I really want to do what is right, but I can't. I do what I don't want to – what I hate. I know perfectly well that what I am doing is wrong, and my bad conscience proves that I agree with these laws I am breaking. But I can't help myself, because I'm no longer doing it. It is sin inside me that is stronger than I am that makes me do these evil things.

> I know I am rotten through and through so far as my old sinful nature is concerned. No matter which way I turn I can't make myself do right. I want to but I can't. When I want to do good, I don't; and when I try not to do wrong, I do it anyway. Now if I am doing what I don't want to, it is plain where the trouble is: sin still has me in its evil grasp.

> It seems to be a fact of life that when I want to do what is right, I inevitably do what is wrong. I love to do God's will so far as my new nature is concerned; but there is something else deep within me, in my lower nature, that is at war with my mind and wins the fight and makes me a slave to the sin that is still within me. In my mind I want to be God's willing servant but instead I find myself still enslaved to sin.

> So you see how it is: my new life tells me to do right, but the old nature that is still inside me loves to sin. Oh, what a terrible predicament I'm in! Who will free me from my

slavery to this deadly lower nature? Thank God! It has been done by Jesus Christ our Lord. He has set me free (Rom. 7:15-25).

"I get it!" The reason I never could have inner peace through my effort was that I did not have it in me to be good – not good enough for God's standards. I wanted to be good. I tried hard to be good, but I also knew my doubts, inner struggles, and failures. I knew that God's law condemned me rather than proved my worth. Where was my hope? It was, it is, in Christ.

This understanding of Jesus Christ as central and pre-eminent in knowing and being accepted by God has kept me in line through a spiritual pilgrimage that, quite frankly, should have veered off course many times. Should I doubt the necessity of salvation (that is, question whether our sins are really that bad), I think of his work on the cross and know that such a sacrifice would only have been made if salvation was necessary. When I doubt the love of God, again, I look to the cross that speaks to me of a love beyond my imagination. When I doubt God's justice, there again I contemplate the cross that mysteriously brings together his mercy and justice. When I doubt there is more to life than what I see, I look to the cross and Christ's resurrection and his ascension, and my heart cannot help but be stirred by the hope of my Lord's return in glory.

It is not a system of belief that keeps me steady. It is the person of Jesus Christ, and the heart of every follower stirs at the same thought. A popular movie that came out at the time of this writing was *Amazing Grace*, the story of William Wilberforce's effort to end the slave trade in the British Empire. Viewers will take away different scenes that particularly struck them, but I can guarantee that everyone who has experienced the saving work of Christ will remember John Newton's line: "I am a great sinner and Christ is a great Savior!"

Oddly enough, I believe Newton's hymn "Amazing Grace" is popular outside the Christian faith because it does not mention the name of Christ or use the term "sin." Thus, anyone can sing the song to express how they have come through tough times. But Newton was referring to himself as a sinner saved by God's grace through Jesus Christ. Here is another hymn Newton wrote that clearly states the place of Christ in his heart, in mine, and in the heart of every believer:

> How sweet the name of Jesus sounds
> In a believer's ear.
> It soothes his sorrows, heals his wounds
> And drives away his fear.
>
> It makes the wounded spirit whole
> And calms the troubled breast;
> 'tis manna to the hungry soul
> And to the weary rest.
>
> Dear name! the rock on which I build,
> My shield and hiding place;
> My never-failing treasury filled
> With boundless stores of grace.
>
> By Thee my prayers acceptance gain
> Altho' with sin defiled;
> Satan accuses me in vain
> And I am owned a child.
>
> JESUS! my Shepherd, Husband, Friend,
> My Prophet, Priest and King;
> My LORD, my Life, my Way, my End,
> Accept the praise I bring.
>
> Weak is the effort of my heart
> And cold my warmest thought;
> But when I see Thee as Thou art
> I'll praise Thee as I ought.

'till then I would Thy love proclaim
With every fleeting breath;
And may the music of Thy name
Refresh my soul in death.

Chapter 2
What Matters is Living by Faith

I had two stumbling blocks to get over in my spiritual pilgrimage, both having to do with faith. If asked what it meant to be a Christian or how one is to be saved, I knew the answer as well as most people in the church – believe in Jesus and try to live a good life. And I did try. I was as good a boy as anyone I knew. I did not "sow wild oats" at any age. I did not drink, smoke, take drugs, tell dirty stories, or swear. I treated people nicely. I was religious. I placed nothing on my Bible and even read it through once. I memorized the Child's Catechism. I worked at being good so that I could be accepted by God.

Yet I lacked assurance of God's acceptance. I remember watching Billy Graham on TV and hearing him proclaim, "I know I am saved!" "Sure," I thought, "You are Billy Graham. Of course you will be saved." I was not a Billy Graham. I was a timid boy who had done nothing great for God. I never was sure if I was keeping all the commandments the way I should. I could not tell if my good deeds outweighed my bad deeds, not that I was noticeably bad; I just couldn't be sure if I was good enough. Finally, at a Billy Graham Crusade of all places, I caught on...for the most part. Salvation is by faith, not by works. I needed to believe in Jesus, what he did for me.

Other experiences helped push me past this stumbling block of faith. Soon afterwards, I met the Christian band who impressed on me that the focus of my faith is to be on Christ himself. Salvation was not about an impersonal faith in doctrine; it was about true faith in the person of Jesus Christ. The experience at Explo'72 all the more impressed on me the central role of faith.

And yet, the concept of living by faith remained a stumbling block, this time for *keeping* good relations with God. I did not have to travel very far along the Christian path before discovering that the trip would be more challenging than I had realized. It was not that the road seemed steep but that I easily grew weary. I needed to renew my faith periodically to keep up the zeal and prove to God I loved him. As time went on I was surprised to find old sins sneaking back into my life. What was wrong with me? What kind of gratitude was I showing Christ for all that he had done for me? I needed to be more committed. I needed more discipline in my religious duties. I should be out evangelizing more.

These nagging worries eventually took another twist – from what's wrong with me to what's wrong with God. Why will God not do more in my life? I am a minister. I work hard to serve God. Why doesn't he produce more results? And then the question became clear: What good is faith? Yes, it gets us salvation but then what? If my life is nearly the same as before, if I am seeing no miracles, and I struggle in my own Christian walk, what good is faith? This discontent with God left me feeling even guiltier and annoyed with myself.

It was preparing a sermon in Mark 5:24-34 that led me to my next "I get it" moment. The passage presents the story about a woman healed from a sickness by touching Jesus' garment. Jesus tells her, "Your faith has made you well." There was my troubling puzzle, not only staring me in the face but actually challenging me to respond. What good is faith? Will it heal the sick or not? Will it move mountains or not?

I turned to Hebrews 11. It depressed me as it spoke of all the great things that men and women were able to accomplish by faith. Then I read the summary in verses 32-40:

> And what more shall I say? For time would fail me to tell of Gideon, Barak, Samson, Jephthah, of David and Samuel and the prophets-- who through faith conquered kingdoms, enforced justice, obtained promises, stopped the mouths of lions, quenched the power of fire, escaped the edge of the sword, were made strong out of weakness, became mighty in war, put foreign armies to flight. Women received back their dead by resurrection.

I did not find any of these examples comforting. I was not conquering kingdoms; I was not risking and then escaping death miraculously. None of my prayers kept a person mortally ill from death, much less raise anyone from the dead. But the passage continues:

Some were tortured, refusing to accept release, so that they might rise again to a better life. Others suffered mocking and flogging, and even chains and imprisonment. They were stoned, they were sawn in two, they were killed with the sword. They went about in skins of sheep and goats, destitute, afflicted, mistreated-- of whom the world was not worthy--wandering about in deserts and mountains, and in dens and caves of the earth.

This gave me pause. Here were believers who did not "succeed." They did not escape death, nor were they raised from the dead. They suffered and did not win victory against their foes. Then came the clincher:

And all these, though commended through their faith, did not receive what was promised, since God had provided something better for us, that apart from us they should not be made perfect.

What is the common element here? Both the "victors" and the "non-victors" were commended for their faith. What did faith accomplish for both? The light came on: It kept them faithful. What is the purpose of faith in our lives? To keep us faithful to God. And it is being faithful to God that matters.

It all began to make sense to me. What is it that I really want to be able to say on my deathbed? I was not inspired by being able to say, "As I look back over my life, I thank God that I was spared any great struggle. Everything went well for me." No, I wanted to say, "I have gone through good and difficult times. There have been many struggles, but I am glad I can say I have remained faithful to my God." Even unbelievers understand this principle, that what makes life worth living is to remain true to what one holds dear. As Don Quixote sang of his quest: "And I know if I'll only be true to this glorious quest, then my heart will lie peaceful and calm when I'm laid to my rest."[1] If the secular world could understand this concept, surely I as a Christian could. What more did I desire than to hear my Master say to me when he greets me, "Well done, good and faithful servant" (Matt. 25:21)?

The context of that verse is the parable of the talents, in which a master gives to his servants different amounts of coins to invest for him. Each servant is measured according to what he is given. My mistake all along had been to measure myself against others with the gifts and abilities given to them. Even then I did not understand the role of circumstances which enhanced or interfered with a person's growth and service, and which were controlled by the providence of God. I worked under the assumption that because faith accomplished great things, the measure of my faith could be determined by the "success" of my ministry.

But now I understood: What matters is by faith to be faithful to God in all circumstances. It is to remain devoted to his service, neither allowing prosperity to lead one astray in pride nor giving in to despondency in adversity.

One other lesson about faith struck me in the same way as this lesson about faithfulness. This time I was sitting in my usual chair on Tenth's pulpit platform listening to Dr. Boice preach. "I know what God wants," he said. (That caught my attention. That really is the question we should be asking and the answer we should most want to know.) "God wants to be believed."

"I get it!" The essence of faith is not believing *in* God as much as it is *believing* God. I believe in God because I believe him. I trust God because I believe what he says. This is why God takes our faith personally. To accept or reject the Gospel as his Word is to accept or reject what he has given and spoken.

This understanding steadied my spiritual walk. One of my ongoing worries was whether or not I would remain faithful to God. Given my weakness, how could I know I would not give up the walk? I know now I will make it to the end. Why? Because "he who began a good work in [me] will bring it to completion" (Phil. 1:6). When reading such a verse before, I might have said to myself, "I hope so. I am such a weak believer." That may sound like a humble thought, but in truth it is arrogance. What I was really saying to God was, "I hope you are right. I am a tougher case than most, and I don't know if you are up to the job." Understanding this insult has time and again stopped me in my tracks when I begin to express a "humble" doubt about what Scripture plainly teaches.

What matters with faith is to remain faithful to God. And what faith places its hope in is the God who is faithful to his word.

Chapter 3
What Matters is Trusting God's Word

"Listen to what the Spirit is saying," our small group leader said quietly as we stood in a circle praying, some breaking out with a "thank you, Jesus" and others speaking in tongues. Then one participant received a word from God. The Lord wanted us to kneel. So we kneeled. I can't remember if anyone else received a word that time, but I was fascinated by the way people in my Charismatic community regularly received messages from God.

"God told me to move my family here."

"God told me to take this job."

"The Lord wants us to sing this song."

They had no doubt they were hearing God, not audibly, but they knew when his Spirit was speaking to their spirit. They might even argue with God about what he wanted of them, but like Jonah, they would eventually have to give in. They might doubt God was right in what he had to say, but they never doubted that he was saying what they heard.

I admire these brothers and sisters of faith who were zealous to live for God as a community. Their prayers were marked by praise and thanksgiving, not the petitions of my tradition. The way I learned prayer was to briefly thank God, next ask him to make me more thankful, and then move on into everything else I wanted to ask for. They would get caught up praising God. Their petitions, if they had any, would come much later. They studied religious principles and ways to serve God. They especially focused on how to love one another.

Yet, their weakness was in studying Scripture. In my small group, we studied topics in which we would use the Bible for help, but we never studied a Bible text. I introduced the concept at one meeting when it was my turn to lead. While chatting before the study began, a friend asked what the lesson would be. I replied that I did not know. I had the Bible text, and we would find out together what the lesson would be. We had an interesting discussion, but the novel idea did not catch on.

Even so, though I thought I understood the importance of knowing God's Word, it was later, after I had moved away, before the light came on. I was still intent on hearing a word from the Lord. The irony of my endeavors is expressed well by the author of a book on punctuation. While she was sitting at a table autographing her books, a woman came up to her bemoaning that though she desperately wanted to know how to punctuate properly, there was nowhere to turn. The author writes, "I said again that the book really did explain many basic things about punctuation; she said again that the basic things of punctuation were *exactly* what nobody was ever prepared to explain to an adult person."

I was in the same position, standing in front of the Holy Spirit with his Book laid open before me and bemoaning that I could not hear a Word from the Lord!

Me: "Give me a word from the Lord!"

Holy Spirit: "Here it is. I've written it in this book."

Me: "Really, I want to know what God has to say."

Holy Spirit: "I have written it all down. Read!"

Me: "Maybe someone has written a good book on the subject."

I eventually came to Tenth Presbyterian Church and sat under the teaching of James Montgomery Boice. He, of course, was noted for expository preaching; yet, it was his conviction of the sufficiency of Scripture for knowing God and living for God that would rub off on me and stabilize my spiritual wavering. I had wanted to hear God speak to me because I wanted to know with certainty what I should be doing. That attracted me to my Charismatic brethren. They were not baffled by what to do. God told them in their inward spirits and sometimes through prophecy. All they had to do was listen. For some reason, though, I could not hear as they did. What I learned from Dr. Boice was that God had already spoken plainly. I needed to open my Bible and read God's Word.

As time went on under his influence, this concept about Scripture steadily sank into my consciousness, but as with my grasping the role of faith, so grasping the place of Scripture hit me in another "I get it" moment. Dr. Boice had invited

Dick Lucas to present a pre-PCRT (Philadelphia Conference on Reformed Theology) seminar on preaching. Though serving as a school principal at the time, I was allowed to attend. As the day went on, I saw that all the speaker was doing was leading us through a series of Bible studies. We would sit around in groups and discuss a passage until we arrived at its meaning.

"I get it!" I said to myself later in the afternoon. What matters is knowing what God's Word actually says. That is what preaching is supposed to do – explain what God is saying in his Word. And what God says in his Word is what his people need to hear. I did not need to work myself up into an emotional state so as to hear the Spirit speaking to my inner spirit; nor did I need to receive a "prophetic word" from a prophet. I needed to open God's written revelation and read it! It was there in Scripture that I could confidently say, "The Lord told me."

Once the light came on, the rest of Dr. Boice's emphasis on expository preaching made sense. The true biblical expositor not only believes that we must know what Scripture has to say, but we must take to heart what Scripture says is important to know. Like so many Christians, I believed that truth was found in the Bible. That is why I read the Bible. But I was unknowingly setting the agenda for Scripture. I decided what I needed to know and then turned to Scripture to find the answers. What I learned through Dr. Boice was that I need to give my attention to systematically reading and studying Scripture without setting agendas for what I was to learn. Let the Holy Spirit, through what he has already written, determine what I need to receive.

That is why we must not only *read* Scripture but read it *systematically*. There is a place to look through the Scriptures for help on a topic or theme. But our greatest benefit comes from reading the books of the Bible. Such reading prevents us from taking verses out of context and saying what they do not really mean. Positively, it gives us clearer insight into what the verses do mean. But what I really came to realize was that by systematically reading the Bible personally, and teaching it in the same way publicly, I was truly doing what I had been pretending to do –

that is, I was seeking a word from the Lord. And I was more likely to get that word because God set the agenda. The Holy Spirit had already written the words of Scripture; he had already determined what needed to be said. Now it was my task to study and listen.

Furthermore, because the words were written, I could have greater assurance of what the Lord was saying! I learned at the Charismatic community that when anyone said the Lord spoke to them, they had not experienced anything different from other Christians who will say more cautiously, "I think the Lord is leading me to..." Given our sin and emotional make-up, how could anyone say with confidence, "This is what the Lord told me"? The one time I can say assuredly, "Thus says the Lord," is when I am reading his written Word. If I look to the written Word for a message from God, I will get it! Not only can I be sure it is a "word from the Lord," but I can further know that it is the word he wants me to hear.

I do not mean to oversimplify hearing from God through Scripture. I still have the common problem of hearing what I want to hear from the written Word. Even as I read through a book of the Bible, I am likely to pick out what I think is important and overlook the rest. All the more reason, then, I am to give attention to careful study of the Bible, and not be looking for another revelation. What is written and is before my eyes is enough revelation to spend my life carefully examining even as it examines me. Hebrews 4:12 says, "For the word of God is living and active, sharper than any two-edged sword, piercing to the division of soul and of spirit, of joints and of marrow, and discerning the thoughts and intentions of the heart." Herein lies the beauty and the terror of God's Word. The more I study this "word of God," the more I find that God is examining me, laying open my very heart. No wonder I want to set the agenda. No wonder I need to let the Lord set it for me.

Chapter 4
What Matters Is Taking Joy in God's Glory

I was wary reading the book. The author was making sense, but he seemed to be going too far with his argument. How trustworthy was this guy? So I took the opportunity one day having lunch with the man I did trust, Dr. James Boice, to ask the question: "I am reading *Desiring God.* What do you think of John Piper?"

Here is Piper's thesis in the book: The chief end of man is to glorify God *by* enjoying him forever. I highlighted some of the sentences from his book:[2]

> ...it is unbiblical and arrogant to try to worship God for any other reason than the pleasure to be had in him (p. 16).

> Praising God, the highest calling of humanity and our eternal vocation, did not involve the renunciation but rather the consummation of the joy I so desired (p. 19).

My aim is to own up to the amazing, and largely neglected, fact that some dimension of joy is a moral duty in all true worship and all virtuous acts (p. 20).

This insistence on personal joy being a necessary element in glorifying God pushed my sensibilities. If glorifying God is what matters most, then I should not value highly my personal pleasure, I had reasoned. Did Jesus not root discipleship in the concept of denying oneself? Piper addresses this question by quoting another author, C. S. Lewis, from whom he learned the principle of joy.

> The negative ideal of Unselfishness carries with it the suggestion not primarily of securing good things for others, but of going without them ourselves, as if our abstinence and not their happiness was the important point. I do not think this is the Christian virtue of Love. The New Testament has lots to say about self-denial, but not about self-denial as an end in itself. We are told to deny ourselves and to take up our crosses in order that we may follow Christ; and nearly every description of what we shall ultimately find if we do so contains an appeal to desire (p. 17; quoting from "The Weight of Glory").

So back to my lunch with Dr. Boice and my question. He replied, "Piper is so scriptural." His point, which would have mattered most for him, was that Piper drenched his writing in Scripture. I went back to the book, this time paying attention to the Scripture quotes.

Delight yourself in the LORD,
and he will give you the desires of your heart (Ps. 37:4).

O, taste and see that the Lord is good! (Ps. 34:8).

How sweet are your words to my taste,
sweeter than honey to my mouth! (Ps. 119:103).

...in your presence there is fullness of joy;
at your right hand are pleasures forevermore (Ps. 16:11).

...the Almighty will be your gold
and your precious silver (Job 22:25).

Somehow I had missed the import of taking pleasure in God. I thought that what mattered was to do one's duty for God regardless of feeling; indeed, what proved true love for God was to serve him when there was no pleasure. Is that not true commitment? Was Jesus feeling happy in

Gethsemane? But that is exactly where Piper and Lewis would press their argument. There is a pleasure deeper than fun feelings; there was a joy for the Son in pleasing his Father in the midst of his suffering.

I thought of my own position as a father. I have two daughters now grown. Suppose I had asked each to clean up their rooms. They both are obedient and get to work. The first takes me to her room when she is done and with a stoic expression says, "Father, you can see that I have cleaned my room. It was a lot of work, but I want to be an obedient daughter and do what is right." I would appreciate her obedience, knowing that she cleaned her room not out of pleasure but still from a desire to show me due respect. The second daughter, when she is done, grabs my arm and pulls me into her room. "See, Dad, what I've done! Do you like it? I want so much to please you!" I would indeed be happy, not by the condition of the room but by the joy my daughter took in wanting to please me. "I get it!" What matters to God is that his people take delight in him!

It all began to make sense. The very notion that God is to be glorified presumes that God is worth glorifying. How then can we glorify him indifferently or begrudgingly? Indeed, this very concept of "bearing one's cross" as though it is an emotional disposition for a Christian to display is what has turned many away from following Christ. They look upon Christians as sour pusses who do not have fun, nor want anyone else to have fun. And that is how many Christians are. They are like the elder brother in "The Prodigal Son" story who serve out of duty and have forgotten the joy that first won them to Christ, if such joy had ever happened to them. The Christian life becomes a set of rules to follow to be dutiful children. They lose the joy that was set before Jesus, which moved him to endure the cross and despise the shame (cf. Heb. 12:2).

I thought through in greater detail of this matter of giving to God and receiving from him. What had led me to Piper's book in the first place was a question posed to me by a seminary student. One Sunday he gave me an article by Piper asking what I thought of his message. The next Sunday, after reading it, I responded in that, whereas we are called to sacrifice for God, the truth is that he out-gives us.

In other words, God gives more to us than we give to him.

But now I asked myself, "When do I ever give to God what he needs?" What have I ever done that God would respond, "Thank you, Marion. What would I have done without you?" Then why does he give me work to do? Is not the very service itself a privilege? And is not that privilege real joy? Do I not delight in the very concept of serving my Creator and King? Do I not find joy taking part in the great enterprise of Christ's Kingdom? My very "giving" is the gift that God has given me. The artist does not bemoan having to create art so as to live. He does not wish that he could lie around doing nothing. He does not regard whatever pay he gets as recompense for the work; rather, the work is his pleasure and he is thankful for having the gift to do it. As much as our society may prize living the easy life, we know that what we really want is to live the meaningful life, which is what we Christians have been given the joy to do.

We are not pondering the meaning of our existence. We know why we live. Our chief end is to glorify God *BY* enjoying him forever. That enjoyment begins now. He is our joy, our treasure. We rejoice in our redemption because it brings us into right relationship with our God. We are thankful for the Spirit's work of sanctification because it deepens our satisfaction in God. We rejoice in our hope because it promises us the day when we will be with our Lord in glory. We suffer, we sacrifice, we struggle through our sin and frailty because of the joy given now that what happens to us and what we do have meaning. We press on, as the Scriptures say, "toward the goal for the prize of the upward call of God in Christ Jesus" (Phil. 3:14). There is a prize, and that prize is no less than being in the presence of God and receiving his blessing.

And as if redemption and a relationship with Christ were not enough, God gives us meaningful service to do for his glory. It does not matter who we are, what gifts we may have, nor what our circumstance may be. All that we have comes from God and is being used by him for his glory. The trouble I had with suffering and poor circumstances was that they seemed to serve little or no purpose.

Even now I cannot understand why most things happen – either good or bad – but I can believe that the God of the Gospel is the God of glory who is working all things to a glorious end. And he is letting me get on the ride! How can I not take delight in such a God?

As I have noted, it was John Piper who opened my mind to grasp the importance of delighting in the Lord. Even so, it was James Boice who by his teaching, ministry, and eventually his death taught me to delight in God's glory. And so I close with his theme passage:

> Oh, the depth of the riches and wisdom and knowledge of God! How unsearchable are his judgments and how inscrutable his ways!
>   "For who has known the mind of the Lord,
>   or who has been his counselor?"
>   "Or who has given a gift to him
>   that he might be repaid?"
> For from him and through him and to him are all things. To him be glory forever. Amen (Rom. 11:33-36).

Chapter 5
What Matters Is Resting in God's Grace

Shame-ridden, he could not confess his sin. Squirming on the couch, he finally passed over a folded piece of paper with the shameful transgression written down – "I have looked at pornography." It turned out that he had used school computers to access sites.

"Is there anything else?" I asked.

"Yes. When standing at the check-out line in the grocery store, I am tempted by the women's magazines."

I think he half-expected that I would throw him out of the church in disgust. Instead, we discussed what could be done to address his temptation. My answer shocked him as much he thought I would be shocked by his sin. "Here is what I want you to do the next time you are standing in line and feeling the temptation (which, by the way, means you have already sinned). I want you to give thanks to God." His eyebrows rose. "I want you to thank God that even at that moment he loves you as much as he ever has or will. For such is the grace and mercy of your Father."

I explained that his real enemy is Satan, who, though he could not steal his soul, still sought to render him ineffectual in living for God. He could not separate a child of God from his Father, but he could make that child feel estranged from his Father. That is where sin comes in, whatever the form it may take.

The most common reason an individual seeks counsel from me has to do with his or her laboring under guilt. They will come to me saying that they are unsure of their salvation because of a sin that they committed which they did not believe they would ever do or because of a besetting sin that they cannot overcome. "How could a Christian live such a way?" they want to know. My response generally follows along these lines: first, I concur that the sin is bad, and actually worse than they think. Like the tip of an iceberg we see very little of our sin's magnitude. Second, I (nicely) help them to see their arrogance in believing that they could not commit the particular sin that shocked them or that they should so easily overcome a recurring sin. Third, I help them to see Satan's intent, which is to make them feel estranged from God. When a Christian is enmeshed in sin, he or she feels guilty. "How could I commit such a sin?" they wail. "What is wrong with me that I keep giving in?" Under this weight of guilt, they no longer feel that they can fellowship with God or serve him without hypocrisy. Thus, their witness and service for God is made ineffective and their joy in God destroyed. Satan is fine with the Christian feeling guilty as long as that guilt keeps him or her from God. For this reason, I present them with the "shocking" step to take of giving thanks. For if our sins lead us to the mercy of God, then Satan's very purpose of tempting us is thwarted. He wants to separate us from God, not drive us to our heavenly Father.

The biblical passage I will then turn to is Hebrews 4:14-16:

> Since then we have a great high priest who has passed through the heavens, Jesus, the Son of God, let us hold fast our confession.

For we do not have a high priest who is unable to sympathize with our weaknesses, but one who in every respect has been tempted as we are, yet without sin. Let us then with confidence draw near to the throne of grace, that we may receive mercy and find grace to help in time of need.

Unlike the other lessons presented, I cannot recall an "I get it" moment when it comes to grace, though I know that my real understanding did not develop until I came to Tenth Presbyterian Church. James Boice's teaching influenced me, of course, as well as exposure to other teachers he brought in, especially for the PCRT conferences. Michael Horton's description of his move from a works-oriented faith to one that is grace-filled particularly struck a chord with me. There were the people who came to me for counsel expressing the same fears and burdens I had had. Their sins were too grievous for God to forgive. They worried that he was angry with them or that he merely tolerated them as a disappointed father. How odd it was to see people who professed to be saved by the grace of God yet muddle through life as though they had to work to

44

keep God's favor. What was the advantage of even turning to Christ for salvation if one has to keep working to hold on to that salvation? But then, that is how I had unwittingly lived, continually measuring whether or not my work was good enough for God's approval just as I had done before knowing Christ.

It was especially seeing how the grace of God played out in people's lives that affected me. Two believers could go through the same trials, yet one grew only stronger in faith while the other despaired. The difference always had to do with their perspective about grace. The one who believed that what he or she did determined how God would regard them either succumbed to pressure and faltered, or grew proud by their supposedly good performance. The one who rested in God's grace, secure in his or her Lord's mercy, typically weathered the storms that came their way and had an objective, humble view of their gifts. What a difference to meet with a believer who bemoans how difficult life is and then with another who has gone through even greater trials and yet extols the grace and blessings of God.

I began to see more clearly how grace covered my life. In my earlier ministry I worried over being such a poor vessel for God to use. I felt I was too proud of my gifts or too lacking in confidence in God. Either way, I waited for God to lower the boom and discredit such an unworthy servant. But now I learned to marvel in the grace of God precisely because he uses such an unworthy servant as myself.

Before, I bemoaned that little was being accomplished in my ministry because I did not see great works of power taking place. Now, I praise God who by his grace uses the ordinary means of preaching and teaching, of prayer, and of the sacraments to quietly and steadily build faith in weak and sinful hearts. The most effective counsel I give to anyone now who comes to me in distress is to help them see for themselves the grace of God in sustaining and blessing them.

I have learned the truth of Scripture which teaches that my sin but makes God's grace abound all the more (Rom. 5:20) and my weakness magnifies the power of the Lord (2 Cor. 12:9). I have learned, in other words, the Gospel. The good news is that God by his grace has provided the way of salvation. God by his grace has chosen to save me and to do *all* that is necessary to carry me through to the day of glory. He has saved me by grace, and he will sustain me by grace.

It is at the Lord's Table that grace is displayed most clearly to me as I stand behind the table as Christ's representative calling his people to come in their sinfulness to receive the Lord's blessing. I have yet to find more fitting words than those of John Calvin, who directed Communion participants to come to the table with no hope but in the grace of God found in Christ:

> ...let us remember that this sacred feast is medicine to the sick, comfort to the sinner, and bounty to the poor; while to the healthy, the righteous, and the rich, if any such could be found, it would be of no value. For while Christ is therein given us for food, we perceive that without him we fail, pine, and waste away, just as hunger destroys the vigor of the body. Next, as he is given for life, we perceive that without him we are certainly dead. Wherefore, the best and only worthiness which we can bring to God, is to offer him our own vileness, and, if I may so speak, unworthiness, that his mercy may make us worthy; to despond in ourselves, that we may

be consoled in him; to humble ourselves, that we may be elevated by him; to accuse ourselves, that we may be justified by him; to aspire, moreover, to the unity which he recommends in the Supper; and, as he makes us all one in himself, to desire to have all one soul, one heart, one tongue. If we ponder and meditate on these things, we may be shaken, but will never be overwhelmed by such considerations as these, how shall we, who are devoid of all good, polluted by the defilements of sin, and half dead, worthily eat the body of the Lord? We shall rather consider that we, who are poor, are coming to a benevolent giver, sick to a physician, sinful to the author of righteousness, in fine, dead to him who gives life... (*Institutes*, Bk III, Ch 17, Par 42)[3]

I cannot overstate how an understanding of God's grace has impacted my life. For whatever the circumstance of life, I am led to the mercy throne of God. If all is going well and I feel victorious, then I am moved to thank God for granting such grace to a miserable sinner like myself. If I am under a storm of suffering, I look to God who sustains me by grace. When I fall into sin, I am moved all the more to glorify God for such mercy that forgives me and still favors me with redeeming love. Truly such grace is amazing that bestows blessing upon a wretch like me...and you.

Conclusion
Does It Matter?

The pain in her stomach hurt, and she wanted to go home. She did not like the hospital examining room, and she was especially mad at the nurse who gave her a shot. She just wanted to go home and get away from these people who pressed on her stomach and poked her with needles. But instead of taking her home, I carried her down a hall and handed her to a stranger, who carried her away from me. And as she called out "Daddy" to me, I discovered how little I really knew the love of God the Father.

I knew the verses: "For God so loved the world, that he gave his only Son..." (John 3:16); "God shows his love for us in that while we were still sinners, Christ died for us" (Romans 5:8); "In this is love, not that we have loved God but that he loved us and sent his Son to be the propitiation for our sins" (1 John 4:10). Yes, I knew that it was out of love that

God the Father sent his Son, but, after all, it was God the Son, who paid the price!

But I learned better that day. If I could have taken my daughter's place, I would have done so in a heartbeat. Indeed, I knew then that I would willingly die in her place, for it would be easier to take her pain than to watch her undergo it. And then to hear her call out to me, as though I had abandoned her – that was the hardest part to bear. It was that experience which shocked me into knowing how little I know of the love of God. It was hard for me to give up my child to one who was taking her to be healed. What was it for God the Father to give up his Son to his enemies who would kill him? What was it for him to hear his Child ask, "Why have you forsaken me?"

I do not know this love by which God the Father gives up his Only Begotten Son, whom he has loved for all eternity, and who has returned that same love. What wondrous love is this? It is this love displayed at the cross that shatters both my confidence in what I profess to know and my doubts. I don't really know the holiness of God and the horror of sin that make necessary such a terrible price

51

of redemption. I don't really know what justice is that demands such a Sacrifice. And I definitely don't understand the merciful love by which God pays the greatest price to redeem his enemies and make them his children given that *it was not necessary for justice nor for his happiness*. Our death would have been justice. Love between God the Father, the Son, and the Holy Spirit was all that was necessary for God's happiness. Why such love for us? For me? I know enough of my pettiness that disqualifies me from being the object of this divine love. And yet there it is, displayed upon the cross along with justice. Like Job, I say, "I have uttered what I did not understand, things too wonderful for me, which I did not know" (Job 42:3).

Sharper minds can debate the existence of God and tackle the problem of evil. At the cross all that I can do is worship the mystery of my God and his Redemption. This is what matters. Theology – studying God and his work through his written Word – takes us to the mountain peak, not so much to discover what is on the other side as it is to look out into the expanse and see how all the greater is the God we try to imagine. Is this not the experience of the scientists? The more they uncover, the greater the mystery deepens. All the more so is the experience of the theologians who believe what is learned and then lets this faith-knowledge take them to new heights through what they experience.

I have learned what matters because of contemplating life experiences through the lens of Scripture. My own intent in writing these accounts of my spiritual pilgrimage had not been to demonstrate the relevancy of theology. That the lessons I learned corresponded with the five *solas* was a discovery in itself, and I hope they illustrate the impact that theology necessarily has on the Christian life. As I have discovered in my own life and seen replayed in the lives of many others in my pastoral ministry, it is the theological concepts that we grasp or fail to grasp that determine our ability to live in peace, joy, and love.

We can only give what we possess. We can only live what we know. If we know Christ truly, have faith in his work for us, rest on the grace of God, and trust in his revealed Word, then our hearts will rejoice in the glory of God and enable us to give the love that we have in Christ. I pray that my lessons may help you along such a path of knowledge and of hope.

Bibliography

[1] "The Impossible Dream," *Man of la Mancha*

[2] Piper, John – *Desiring God*, Multnomah Books, 2003.

[3] Calvin, John – *Institutes of the Christian Religion*, trans. by Henry Beveridge.

Author Information

D. Marion Clark is a minister in the Presbyterian Church in America. His sermons and writings may be accessed at www.dmcresources.com. He may be contacted at mg79clark@yahoo.com.

Made in the USA
Columbia, SC
12 August 2017